武満 徹

ギターのための

エキノクス

TORU TAKEMITSU
EQUINOX

for guitar

SJ 1090

SCHOTT

4

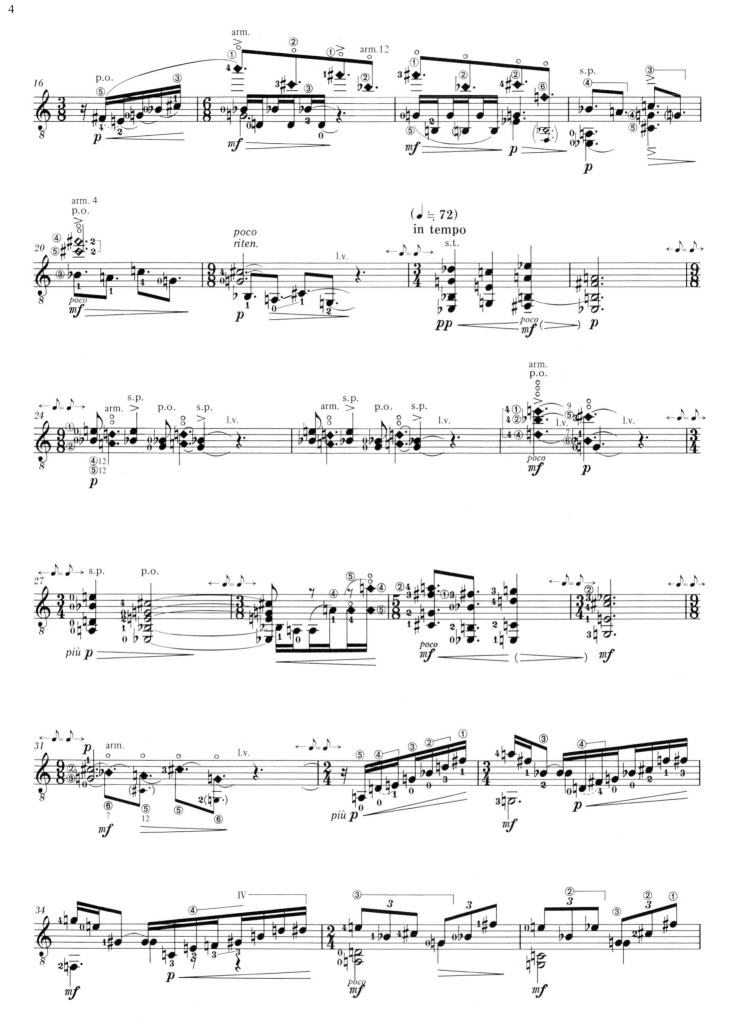

Equinox
エキノクス
for guitar

Toru Takemitsu
Fingerings by Manuel Barrueco

武満 徹
マヌエル・バルエコ 運指

ギターのための《エキノクス》は、荘村清志のデビュー25周年記念リサイタルのために作曲され、彼に捧げられている。
1994年4月4日、東京で、荘村清志によって初演された。

演奏時間——5分

Equinox for guitar was composed for the recital commemorating the 25th anniversary of Kiyoshi Shomura's debut and is dedicated to him.
The first performance was given by Kiyoshi Shomura on April 4, 1994 in Tokyo.

Duration: 5 minutes

ABBREVIATIONS:

s.p.   = sul ponticello
s.t.   = sul tasto
p.o.   = Position (or Play) ordinary
l.v.   = Let vibrate

武満 徹《エキノクス》　　　　　　　　　●

ギターのための

初版発行─────────────────1995年4月5日

第3版第5刷⑧───────────2016年12月12日

発行──────────────ショット・ミュージック株式会社

─────────────東京都千代田区内神田1-10-1 平富ビル3階

─────────────〒101-0047

─────────────(03)6695-2450

─────────────http://www.schottjapan.com

─────────────ISBN 978-4-89066-390-3

─────────────ISMN M-65001-005-4

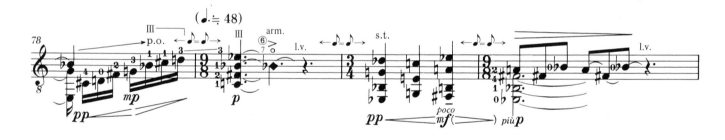

* Left Hand Thumb

現代の音楽
MUSIC OF OUR TIME

武満 徹
Toru Takemitsu (1930–1996)

エキノクス
Equinox
for guitar . . . SJ 1090 . . . 900円

ギターのための12の歌
12 Songs for Guitar
Transcription for guitar
SJ 1095 . . . 2100円

ギターのための小品
——シルヴァーノ・ブソッティの60歳の誕生日に——
A Piece for Guitar
——*For the 60th Birthday of Sylvano Bussotti*——
SJ 1130 . . . 500円

すべては薄明のなかで
——ギターのための4つの小品——
All in Twilight ——*Four pieces for guitar*——
SJ 1051 . . . 2000円

ラスト・ワルツ
The Last Waltz
Transcription for guitar of a work by L. Reed & B. Mason
SJ 1118 . . . 600円

森のなかで ——ギターのための3つの小品——
In the Woods ——*Three pieces for guitar*——
SJ 1099 . . . 1500円

不良少年
Bad Boy
for two guitars . . . SJ 1074 . . . 1200円

ギター重奏曲集
Music for Guitars
SJ 1129 (performing score) . . . 1500円

海へ
Toward the Sea
for alto flute and guitar . . . SJ 1007 (performing score) . . . 1500円

細川俊夫
Toshio Hosokawa (1955–)

恋歌 I
Renka I
for Soprano and guitar
Text from Manyoshu and Shin-kokinshu (in Japanese)
SJ 1066 . . . 1400円

セレナーデ
I. 月光のもとで　II. 夢路
Serenade
I. In the Moonlight II. Dream Path
for guitar . . . SJ 1154 . . . 1200円

ショット・ミュージック株式会社
東京都千代田区内神田1-10-1 平富ビル3階　〒101-0047
電話 (03) 6695-2450　ファクス (03) 6695-2579
sales@schottjapan.com　http://www.schottjapan.com

SCHOTT MUSIC CO. LTD.
Hiratomi Bldg., 1-10-1 Uchikanda, Chiyoda-ku, Tokyo 101-0047
Telephone: (+81)3-6695-2450 Fax: (+81)3-6695-2579
sales@schottjapan.com http://www.schottjapan.com

（価格には消費税が含まれておりません）